Next Time
You Come Home

Also by Lisa Dordal

Mosaic of the Dark
Water Lessons

Next Time You Come Home

Lisa Dordal and Milly Dordal

www.blacklawrence.com

Executive Editor: Diane Goettel
Cover Design: Zoe Norvell
Book Design: Amy Freels
Cover Art: "Winter Garden" by Yuki Lamb

Published 2023 by Black Lawrence Press.
Printed in the United States.

For my mother, Mildred ("Milly") Reinke Dordal
October 1, 1928–April 7, 2001

Contents

Part I

My Mother Returns

My mother died on April 7, 2001, at the age of seventy-two. Twenty years later, in 2021, I rediscovered one hundred and eighty letters she had written to me between 1989 and 2001, plus one from 1983 when I was away at college. My mother had been an avid letter writer, writing two to three times a month when I was in college and then, later, when I lived in San Francisco and Nashville. I had, of course, read all the letters at least once before, when I received them, but it was an entirely different experience to re-read them twenty years after her death.

Not long after I started reading them, my wife walked into our living room to find me sitting on the couch sobbing as if my mother had died that afternoon—and with more emotion than I had expressed at the time of her death. It's not that I didn't grieve when my mother died. But my grief was muted by the fact that, in many ways, my mother had left me long before her actual death. My mother started drinking "regularly"—the word she uses in her 1983 letter—in the mid-1970s, when I was about ten. During the day, she was high functioning: a social worker who hated to put clients on a waiting list; a tireless volunteer at church and in our neighborhood, often serving on several committees at a time; an active participant in the PTA. She also managed a myriad of household tasks, from grocery shopping, cooking, and laundry to window washing and painting. Plus, she had a great sense of adventure and was fun to be around. During one of my college summers—after I had returned from a two-month study-abroad program in the Soviet Union—she researched Russian restaurants in the Chicago area and then took me to lunch at one of them so she and I could enjoy something of my Russian experience together.

I loved my daytime mother. But in the evening, she disappeared. Typically, my mother would start drinking in the late afternoon while preparing dinner, then continue on until bedtime. I remember many dinners when she seemed to look right through me. After college, when I was no longer living at home, I made a point of calling her during the day rather than during the evenings, so I wouldn't have to hear her slurred speech. As the years progressed, she drank more and more until gradually the boundaries between daytime and nighttime blurred. I remember calling at ten one morning, and her speech was already—or maybe still—slurred.

Although my mother did most of her letter writing at night (she frequently includes the time in her headings, as well as the date), it's only my daytime mother who comes through in the letters. There's no slurred speech, no smell of bourbon or vermouth, no clinking of ice cubes inside her coffee mug. And there's no sense of her looking through me. As I re-read the letters, I felt seen in a way I often hadn't when my mother was alive.

As soon as I finished re-reading the letters, I began to think about how I could preserve them. Having lost my daytime mother so many years before, when the boundaries between day and night blurred, the last thing I wanted was to lose her again. I decided that typing up the letters—which were all handwritten—would be better than scanning them because the process of typing would allow me to spend more time with my mother, and in a more participatory and embodied way. My mother wrote long letters—four or five pages long—and I am not a fast typist, so this process took several weeks. I was so worried about something happening to the letters before I finished that I even purchased a metal box in which to put, at the end of each day, the letters I had not yet typed up. At night I stored this metal box next to my nightstand for easy access in the event of an emergency.

I was not consciously aware, during the typing process, of what my next steps would be or even that there would be next steps. But something must have been working inside me at the subconscious level because, right after I finished typing up the letters, I began tinkering with them, distilling each one down from several single-spaced pages to about half a page, and then distilling them more and more. Throughout this process, I deleted a significant amount of text, going from my mother's more than 112,000 words to approximately 12,000 words. Thus, this wasn't a simple editing process; it was more like a sculpting exercise. Everything I needed was there; I just needed to strip away what wasn't necessary. It was similar, I imagine, to the process of shaping something new out of a large mound of clay—stripping away text to let the parts I wanted to keep soar, and rearranging text when I wanted to bring out certain tensions between stories or images.

If someone had asked me, during the distillation process, what criteria I was using to decide what text to keep and what to delete, I'm not sure I would have been able to provide a satisfactory answer. Looking at the final entries, I would say that I seem to have been drawn to observations about the passage of time, about seeing beauty in the natural world, about grief and loss, as well as to those about societal issues such as racism and sexism and even climate change (though she doesn't use that phrase). I also seem to have been drawn to small, ordinary moments such as what my mother was making for dinner on a particular night, what book she was reading for her book club, or who she saw on the way to the grocery store. But at no point did I consciously articulate for myself a set of criteria. Instead, the process felt more like one of deep listening and, in this way, felt very collaborative. My mother provided the words and I provided the shape or distillation.

Throughout the process, I tried to keep my mother's language as close to her original phrasing as possible, and I also kept her unconventional use of capitalization. But I did take some liberties in terms of ordering. Sometimes I placed two thoughts or anecdotes together that didn't originally appear in the same letter—only perhaps in the same general time period—because I felt that the two ideas spoke to each other. And I frequently combined letters from one month into a single entry; this is why the final headings consist only of the month and year. For the 1983 letter, I did the reverse and created two separate entries because the letter was so long. At one point, I experimented with turning every letter into a sonnet, but I soon abandoned this approach because I felt like I was imposing a structure that wasn't in service to my mother's words. I also experimented with different line lengths, in the end opting mostly for longer lines that are end-stopped (i.e., ending with some sort of punctuation) or end-paused (ending without punctuation but in a way that makes sense syntactically). The final entries are, in my view, something *between* letters and poems—not fully letters and not fully poems but, instead, their own thing. Ordinary moments distilled into language that is not only conversational and informative but also, I hope, sharp and luminous.

There are significant sequence gaps in the original letters and thus in the final entries. I have only one letter from my college years, though I know my mother wrote many other letters during that time. I'm not sure when or why I discarded the other letters. However, given that the saved letter is one in which my mother speaks openly about her drinking, it seems clear that saving this letter was intentional. There are also sequence gaps in the letters from 1989 to 2001—entire months that are missing. Other gaps occur (in the narrative of this book) because I opted not to include anything from certain letters in the final sequence, usually because I didn't find anything that I felt needed to be distilled. My approach, arising from my own poetic impulse, was "less is more."

These gaps in the letters, coupled with the fact that the final entries don't fit neatly into one category—not fully poems, not fully letters—to me serve as a lovely metaphor for my relationship with, and understanding of, my mother. There are some things about the past—about my mother's life and the relationship I had with her—that I have access to, but there is much more that I don't. My mother was thirty-six when she gave birth to me—she had a whole rich life before I was born, a life which I'll never have full access to. And now, since her death when I was thirty-six, I've had a whole rich life that she'll never have full access to. Just as my mother will always be (for me) "not fully this, not fully that," so, too, will I be, for her, "not fully this, not fully that."

Throughout the twenty years between my mother's death and my rediscovery of the letters, I had thought that my memories of her had been sufficient to allow me to feel her continued presence in my life. I didn't know anything was missing in terms of my ability to experience her continued presence. I also didn't know that the letters, and everything they represent, had been with me all along. During all those years that my wife and I had lived in our Sylvan Park house at the corner of 38th and Nebraska and then, later, in our Bellevue house near the woods of Percy Warner Park, I had walked in and out of our bedroom without the slightest idea of what lay hidden in the closet. Years during which I wrote research papers for my MDiv program and poems for my MFA program; began my college teaching career; traveled to Glacier National Park, Costa Rica, the Grand Canyon, and Isle Royale; flew to Maine with my wife to legalize our marriage; grew butternut squash, asparagus, and Black-Eyed Susans in our front yard; experienced a failed adoption; grieved the loss of four dogs—all this and more, without my having any idea that my mother, in the form of her letters, was there the entire time.

On a different but related note, I have come to see a parallel between this rediscovery of my mother through her letters and my own deepening of religious faith starting at the age of thirty. During my early experiences of religion—as a child and young adult—my faith was perfunctory. I memorized creeds, attended church regularly, and professed a belief in God, but my faith didn't begin to become heartfelt until I came out of the closet at the age of thirty. It was only in accepting and celebrating myself as a lesbian—after so many years of hating myself—that I was able to begin to feel the presence of a larger love in my life. During my years of reciting creeds and attending church, I thought I had loved God, had *experienced* God, but after my transformation at age thirty, I realized that, previously, I had loved God only superficially. God had been there the entire time, but I had loved God only with my head, not with my heart.

Religious mystics speak of God as always being present: we don't let God in; rather, God is already, and always, there. As Franciscan priest Richard Rohr writes: "You cannot *not* be in the presence of God. There's no other place to be. The only change is always on our side—God is present, but we're not present to Presence" (Daily Meditation: Nov 12, 2021). Similarly, I now see that my mother's love was there all along—even when she was drunk—and has continued to be present since her death. Just as my experience of the Divine has been so much richer since I came out as a lesbian, so too is my experience of my mother's love so much richer than it was before I rediscovered her letters.

In one letter, my mother writes that she wishes she could be more spiritual. My guess is that a deeper sense of spirituality would only have been possible had she dealt with her alcoholism and its underlying causes. Yet I do see something spiritual in her meditative focus on small, ordinary moments. Whether she's searching for her keys, dropped in the snow on her walk home from work; hiking in Yosemite with my father; or listening to a wood thrush singing in the backyard, my mother comes across as being fully present. As busy as she was, there is a deep sense of focus that comes through in her writing, a trait I especially appreciate in this era of the internet and social media, when it's all too easy to lose focus.

Of course, there's no way to know how present my mother actually felt during these experiences. My mother, as the person who wrote these letters, is also the person who drank. But, even so, I have felt guided by her words, by the way she took the time to observe, record, and reflect upon ordinary moments in her life. In this way, her words have encouraged me on my own journey of trying to be more present and to focus, really focus, on what is right in front of me at any given time.

My intention in creating these distillations, though, is not to erase my mother's alcoholism. The letters have revealed for me—have *reminded* me—how much my mother really did love me and see me, but they have also shown me that my categories of "daytime mother" and "nighttime mother" are somewhat misleading. My mother was an alcoholic even when she was clear-eyed (i.e., not actively drinking) during the day. But, as her letters have shown me, she could be clear-eyed (in her writing) even at night after she had been drinking.

At one point, my mother wanted to be a writer—she wrote short stories in high school and college—but she was discouraged early on by someone who told her she would need to write every day, even while juggling a career, a marriage, children, etc. My mother sacrificed her dream of becoming a writer so that she could raise my three siblings and me in a way that instilled in us a deep appreciation for the natural world, a love of adventure, and a desire to make the world a little better than the way we found it. Despite her alcoholism, she modeled what it means to be an engaged citizen and compassionate presence in the world, as well as what a rewarding life can look like—one nourished by intellectual curiosity, life-long relationships with family and friends, and active participation in a religious community.

Thank you, Mom, for your whole-hearted love. I may not always have felt it when you were alive, but I feel it now. Thank you for your writerly eye—for teaching me that "small" moments are not small at all; they are everything we have. And thank you for returning, this time for good.

Love—so much love—now and always,

L.

Part II

Not Fully This, Not Fully That

September 1983

This should arrive in time; I hope the Post Office doesn't disappoint.
I tried to make the cookies as good as the ones we ate
in Atlantic City, but they aren't.

We had a lovely weekend at the Lake over Labor Day—
grilling steaks, bobbing around on inner tubes.
Leah's sister was in town. Have you ever met her? She's pretty
but in a colder, more sophisticated way. I like Leah's prettiness better.

Just now, WFMT played "Blue Skies" by Irving Berlin—
his songs were what I grew up with. Happy songs
in Depression America. Yes, I attended Alfred's funeral.
He was 25. There was a bouquet from his fiancée.

I appreciate the letter you sent. You were 10 when I started drinking,
maybe 9. I've put you through a lot of pain.

The dried blossoms are from the mock orange tree in our yard.
I carry your letter in my purse.

September 1983

It's 9:30 PM. I have one eye on the game—they're tied in the 10th.

Saturday, we attended Bob and Marnie's wedding.
Catholics and Lutherans communed by Catholic dispensation.
We sat with Polly, danced at the reception, and were home by 9.

Do you remember Hans Thurber? We stayed a week with him in '73.
You probably don't remember him. He died, Tuesday, at 53.

Yes, *Newsweek* arrived. I'll send it on. Also, the *Lutheran*.

There was a home invasion last week on 56th, near Blackstone.
The son was killed; the father is at Billings. He thinks his injuries—
severe to his head—are from a bike accident he had in July.

July 1989

You are now being introduced to my father's old invoice paper
that I'm still using up since his demise in '74.

Your apartment sounds nice—
can you really go up to the roof and be outside?

Saturday, we had dinner at Peridot. The food was good
but I didn't like the paint-splashed walls—intended to look
like something French. Our 4th was quiet and didn't feel like the 4th.
We sat on the side porch, listening to the 1812 Overture.

I'm getting anxious about our trip. Hoping to "wing it" in Italy—
we might end up sleeping in train stations.

Erik and Franz were in Chicago last week—
they received a warm welcome from their father.
After no contact since '74, no one knew what to expect.

I'm wearing the gym shoes that you left.

August 1989

I'm home from work; the bells are pealing at Mitchell.

I brought in a dahlia for the vase on my desk
and an earwig crawled out—that made me think of you, so here I am.

I still miss our Wednesday lunches—
and when I pass the yogurt section at Mr. G's, I reach out
to buy one for you. Instead, I get "Cracklin' Oat" cereal for $4.
You left us a partial box and Dad loves it.

I'm glad your earthquake scare wasn't as bad
as the lady in the coffee shop predicted.
Last year, someone calculated that the world would end in '88.
Now he says the world will end on Friday.

Should I send the other box from the back bedroom?
I hope your Tuesday fish turned out okay.

August 1989

Beautiful day here—blue skies, low humidity,
the Cubs are winning. What a strange experience

you had on your first day of work—
I'm glad you didn't go with that woman, outside the office.

Our trip to Italy was ok. The Lake was crowded;
a hail storm dented our car. Germany was beautiful—
flowers everywhere. I already want to go back.

We're making progress—Building & Grounds—
on the churchyard: plaques, type of letters, manner of scattering.

I put the envelope you sent in the top drawer of your dresser.
It feels good to have something in there of yours.

September 1989

It's cold here, suddenly, and two weeks earlier than usual.
I need to make sorrel soup once more before a freeze—
and cut the remaining basil. I had planned to bake cookies today,
but an invasion of spiders altered my plans.
And we'd just heard Kris read *Be Nice to Spiders*
during our visit. It was a real hit.

Did Kris tell you Donna Beeps—David's imaginary friend—
now lives in Alaska? She's left the drawer beneath their kitchen sink.

The day we drove to West Virginia was Pachelbel's birthday—
we must have heard the Canon a dozen times. Everyone enjoyed
seeing your pictures, hearing about your life in San Francisco—
the earthquake, the case of mistaken identity.

October 1989

It's a warm Friday evening—it felt good to work outside,
planting bulbs and cleaning up the garden. The sky
was so blue and the temperature, in the 70s.

Yesterday, I ran into Jackie. She's making pillows with a friend—
they're being marketed at several Michigan Avenue stores.

Your mattress has ended up with a Hungarian family—
a mother, father, two boys. One boy is at Ray, the other, Kenwood.

Did you see the *New Yorker* article
about the endangerment of all life, including humans?

Marcella has been voted Senior Queen of Porter County.
The paper said she is 71.

Last week—with the Earthquake—was difficult.
Those few days—Tues, Weds, Thurs—seemed an eternity.
Everyone has been asking about you.

November 1989

I feel like I have a new wardrobe, thanks to you. Rockport shoes,
a flannel shirt. Today I'm wearing the blue and white checked sweater.

Sunday, Dad and I put up the Christmas lights.
Leonard said we go higher every year.

Your hiking boots are on their way. The mountains should be beautiful.
Tell us where you go, so I can follow you on the map.

I see you asked for my split pea soup recipe—
there's usually one on the bag of peas. I add dry vermouth
and bouillon, if I have it.

Your Nov 1st tradition ties in nicely with All Saints Day,
when it's customary to visit the cemetery.
In Mexico, I understand, people decorate the graves with marigolds—
or *Mary's gold*.

December 1989

Do you ever get tired of my odds and ends of stationery?
I hope not, as there is lots more.

I love the turtleneck you sent—did you know it was made in Malawi?
There was a *New Yorker* article recently about Malawi.
And Carl, from church, just began two years of Peace Corps there.

It doesn't feel like New Year's Eve—
dinner is in pans, ready to heat. It's drizzly and slippery—
grey sky, grey earth.

Last week, I fixed Lutefisk for Dad and Leonard.
They ate nearly five pounds.

January 1990

It's cold here—not a day to be outside.
I envied your hiking around.
I'm sorry Dad and I didn't have a better map when we were there—
the lake we hiked to was all dried up.

How did the ordination go?
The *New York Times* had an article about your church.

Next week, we have one more opera, *Hamlet*.
Tomorrow it's *Ghosts* by Ibsen (at Court Theater).

Do you remember the restaurant we went to after shopping at Margie's?
It has gone out of business. The owner got mixed up in cocaine.

February 1990

Dad and I are watching the unabridged version of the *Wizard of Oz*—
a special for the 50th anniversary. No one thought it would be a hit.

This morning, my dermatologist removed two "spots" on my lip
with liquid nitrogen—for $100! I wish I'd done it myself
with the dry ice that comes with our Christmas steaks.

I love the "Broken Pitcher" notecard you sent.
The woman in the painting reminds me of you (and me).

Silly Putty is 40 years old this week.
To celebrate, they are making it in colors.

I finished Beverly Cleary's *A Girl from Yamhill*.
She had such an unhappy childhood.
How could she write such funny stories?

March 1990

The leaky faucet upstairs just "gave way"—water is pouring out—
one of the things the plumber was to fix, but he never showed.

We now have an Osco Pharmacy in Hyde Park—
and, soon, we'll have a Rose Records on 53rd and a funeral home.
Both are needed.

Have you ever read *The Learning Tree* by Gordon Parks?
It's very descriptive of what it was like to be Black in Kansas,
fifty years ago. Perhaps it still is. Yesterday,

I found a seed catalog offering the early yellow flower
in your former landlady's garden—Winter Aconite—
and placed an order for fall delivery.

Dad and I are doing another tax appeal—
if I win, I'll treat myself to a Hearts of Palm salad.

The circus, on Sunday, was disappointing. The bears seemed tired.
I agreed they needed to be hibernating.

April 1990

The plumbing problem is now repaired, at a cost
of $800. Every plumber tells me our pipes could give way any time.
Dad doesn't hear me.

Your flight information is posted on the refrigerator.
We look forward to 6/9 and will mourn 6/22.
I was hoping the roses and clematis would be in bloom when you're here,
but everything is ahead of schedule.

Yesterday, I saw a black-hooded warbler—
that, plus the black-capped green warbler make two firsts for my list.

The Sand Hill Crane is looking at me from the Audubon Calendar.
That's a spectacular bird. We've seen it when it migrates.

Draw me a picture of your Oak chairs, so I can picture you
sitting, writing, reading in them—

June 1990

The week you were here went much too fast.
David says the best thing about Chicago was "doing grandma's jobs"—
not the boat ride or the zoo or Mt. Baldy.

Wednesday, I went downtown for the Frank Lloyd Wright exhibit.
They had four chairs we could sit in. Two were awful.
I'd never sat in a Frank Lloyd Wright chair before.

The back porch is now repaired (by Ed) and painted (by me).

I'm sad your rent is so high, but having a living room—
and a bedroom—sounds like a healthy (mental) investment.

The sky right now is a beautiful mix of purple and pink.

I've thought lots about the Frederick Buechner quote you sent.

July 1990

I've enjoyed our many calls, but I miss writing—so, here I am.

This morning, I let myself sleep in—
feeling the breezes through the screen and listening to the rain.
For breakfast, I made sausage and biscuits.
You know how that reminds me of your summer
working in the Rockies; and then I miss you all over again.

Last week, Dad and I purchased a CD player; we were like kids
with a new toy, rushing out to buy four CD tapes at Rose Records.

Sunday, we went to the Goodman to see *The Gospel at Colonus*—
the Oedipus story played out in gospel music, with a Pentecostal setting.

I bought a frame for my San Francisco picture.
It's going to my LSTC office.

August 1990

It's hot here—92 degrees, high humidity.
Yesterday, I weeded for an hour and came in red-faced and sweaty.

This morning, I was Deacon at church.
Larry is away. Phil preached. He's a sweetheart,
but wasn't sure of the procedures.
After the offering, he kept sitting on the sedilium.
Plus, he substituted John for Matthew
and I had to read nearly an entire chapter.

Peter and Peg invited us over for dinner tonight,
but Dad insisted they come here. So, I insisted that he
(Dad) go to Mr. G's to buy a second chicken.
He confessed he'd never bought one before.
I see I've been too protective of his time.

I'm sure by now you've read that Nolan Ryan pitched his 300th game.

September 1990

Dad and I are having a "sundowner" on the side porch,
waiting for ribs to finish on the grill.

Thank you for your gifts and card. The Quimper napkins are beautiful.
I'll never be able to use them.

Our new Campus Minister is a woman—
she presided yesterday for the first time.
I think we'll all benefit from her worship style.

Jackie and her girls stayed in Beverly Shores last week.
She always leaves the house very clean and
very rearranged. She puts away the dish pan,
bathroom rug, etc. I used to be annoyed.

Now I appreciate the adventure of finding things
in unexpected places. It's like being on a Treasure Hunt,
when we first arrive.

November 1990

It's cold here and we have frost.
Most of the leaves have fallen or turned color.

I worked this afternoon. Dad picked up his slot machine
which was repaired. It looks great but broke again
just after I put in the seventh nickel.
Dad is not in a good mood about that.

I'm sorry I can no longer look forward to our visit.
I had that image before us all summer.
But now I can look back to memories.

I especially needed to see where you live—
to know that it is warm and cozy. It is every bit of that.
I'd enjoy working in your kitchen,
looking out the window in your living room,
sitting on your purple sofa.

January 1991

We started dismantling the tree yesterday.
After taking off 150 ornaments, I quit, had a glass of wine,
and wrote a letter at my desk.

Today we completed the task. As usual,
the needles clogged the vacuum.

I just put a chicken pot pie in the oven.
We'll eat in an hour. I can hear Dad,
through the intercom, shooting pool downstairs.

Outside is a winter fairyland.

The Middle East has me worried.
Bush is determined. Congress has caved.
It will not be a short war.

April 1991

Today is sunny and the birds are coming back.
Three downy woodpeckers—one male and two females—
are at the suet feeder. Goldfinches, juncos, and chickadees
are in and out of the yard.

Last night, I watched *The Grapes of Wrath* on PBS.
The TV made it more tragic for me—seeing everything at close range.
I did enjoy the music.

Do you buy Sleepy Time Tea? On each box, there's a quotation
from a noted author. You're supposed to copy the quotation
(for their contest) and mail it in. I stood in the aisle at Dominick's
and copied the shortest one I could find.

P.S. I'm thrilled you're drying your paper towels and using them twice!

May 1991

It's like a summer day here—really, a little too warm.
Dogwood, lilacs, and columbines are in bloom.
The birds were so noisy, they woke me up at 5 AM.
There must be several wren nests near our house.

In Costa Rica, I spotted a white-necked puffbird on an open branch.
After that, everyone in our group called me the "bird lady."
The country is beautiful—it is compared to Switzerland.
The central valley has mountains, fields of coffee, bananas, cows.
In Carara Park, we spotted a large troop of white-faced monkeys.
The food was okay. I grew to love the rice and red beans.
We did feel aftershocks. There are 105 volcanoes,
and earthquakes are common.

I'm feeling very sad about Bangladesh. Also, Henry Russe—
he died, yesterday, of a heart attack. He was 63.

May 1991

It's been a blurry week. Sheila died on Thursday,
the funeral was Monday.

I find myself remembering her in so many different ways—
yesterday, I used the white purse she'd given you.

Sheila never accepted me as a social worker.
Working part-time, I could say "no" to cases.
No wonder she always gave me bath salts for my birthday—
she saw me as a lady of leisure.

When we moved into the house, we did things together—
like go to a Martin Luther King rally.
Or we'd have a glass of wine together while I fixed supper.

The relationship changed after she married,
but we were always friends.

June 1991

I'm at my desk—looking out at the Unitarian Church—
wondering what you're doing.

The Bulls are playing game two here. I hope they win.

It's been a pleasant day—putting screens in place,
washing windows, planting gladiolas, dahlias, and lilies.
The clematis and two rose bushes are in bloom.

Your cooking adventures sound wonderful—I wish Dad liked lentils.

Heavy rain on Saturday turned to sunshine on Sunday.
We hiked the beach in Beverly Shores.

(The Bulls just won. It was a great game.)

John is doing ok. He's sorting Sheila's clothes
and throwing things away.

July 1991

I'm on the side porch watching the fireflies.
It's in the 90s here, with no rain forecast.

Monday—when Dad learned he no longer had a job—
was difficult. So much of his identity has been wrapped up in his work.
He can't just stop and take up gardening and house repair.
It will force many changes on me, as well.

Our computer at LSSI finally arrived.
It's been promised for over a year. Now it sits in a box on the floor.

I finished reading *Iron John*. Dad read two chapters
and decided it isn't for him. I'm glad I read it—
the movement is popular among the male students at LSTC.

I haven't had a chance to speak to Larry yet
about a series on Goddess worship, but I hope to soon.

August 1991

The days have been warm, the nights cool. However,
no rain. Trees are stressed, grass is brown,
no tomatoes, corn farmers are having a hard time.

Today, before work, I biked to 47th Street.
The Lake was gorgeous and green.

The chemical spill in the Sacramento River sounds terrible.
And now those oil tankers polluting the Olympic Rain Forest.
It goes on and on.

It still seems strange that Dad is home every day—
and difficult, as when he rearranges the kitchen cupboards.
It can get testy.

August 1991

I'm on the side porch, sipping a Manhattan.
For dinner, we had the split pea soup I'd made earlier from a hambone.

Your letter arrived Friday—
it's always nice to come home from work to find a letter.

Next month, we're going to Beverly Shores for vacation—
then on to Charleston, Beaufort, and Savannah.

Last Sunday, we went to the Art Institute for an exhibit
on Degenerative German Art—the *avant-garde*
artists, writers, and musicians who Hitler disliked.

A terrible time in history. Being of German background,
I don't want to identify myself with it.
But I have to.

August 1991

Saturday, we picked up Harold's chicken and took the #6 downtown
for a concert and the Venetian Night boat parade.
The concert was excellent. The boat parade was a bit tacky.
It was more fun to wait in the toilet line—
we joked and laughed for half an hour.

The group arrives on Sunday; we'll celebrate David's 6th birthday.
Isn't that hard to believe?
His baptism is such a vivid event.

I hope your camping trip worked out.
Peter and Andrew invited us to tag-along to Devil's Lake.
Dad hasn't wanted to camp for years—
but he's agreed!

September 1991

It's birthday time in the family—
I wish we could be with you. Your packages are in the mail.
I'm sure the cookies will be crumbs,
but they were sent with love.

When Kris was here, we ate a simple perch dinner
at a restaurant in Michigan City, right on the Lake.
Boats went by, ducks came to the walkway.
At 7:15, an Amtrak train came through on the bridge.
David was mesmerized. You probably went over that bridge
when you took the train to West Virginia.

My 45th high-school reunion was fun.
Some of us have grown apart. Others, I connected with.
It was a bit frantic at the opening banquet—
trying to find former friends based on name tags.

October 1991

We walked our way through Charleston,
touring 17th and 18th century houses,
concluding with a candlelight walk.

Today we drove to Beaufort where we learned more history
of the old south. Then on to Hilton Head—

boring and affluent. I had hoped to visit Daufuskie Island,
settled by freed slaves from Sierra Leone, but the causeway was out.
Tonight, we're in another restored city.

The weather has been wonderful—no storms, no humidity.
The leaves in West Virginia were stunning.

David made me blueberry muffins, from scratch,
for my birthday. We visited his school one day,
and watched him get on and off the bus.

October 1991

It's Saturday afternoon. I'm at the little writing table in Beverly Shores
with a cup of tea resting on my "In Vino Veritas" coaster.

The weather, last night, turned nasty. 30 MPH winds,
temps in the 20s. I'm grateful we have the storm windows on.

This morning, we drove to Sears to look at microwaves.
We had a noisy argument in the car but behaved ourselves at Sears
and seem to be heading toward a compromise.
Another couple our age was also buying their first one,
mainly for White Castle "sliders."

Last Thursday, one of my favorite secretaries dropped dead.
She'd had lunch with other staff and had felt fine—then collapsed
while talking to a student. It has brought Sheila's death very close again.

November 1991

Yesterday, I turned on Leonard Bernstein's *Candide*
for a break during daytime chores and couldn't turn it off.
I never realized the irony of his adaptation—
that it was a reaction to the McCarthy era.

The Thomas hearings really upset me—
all those white male faces discounting Hill's testimony.
I'm sorry he was confirmed. She's the victim, not him.

Your eggplant parmesan sounded delicious.
To me, it's a meal, with a salad. But if I make it for Dad,
I have to make something else with meat.

The new Chicago library has opened to rave reviews.

We're hanging in there with Talman. Don't worry too much.

How was bird watching? What did you see?

December 1991

We're home from Symphony.
Snow came just as we were heading down; driving was slippery.

The music was loud and dissonant, but the *Tribune*
(Von Rhein) gave a positive review. Did I tell you
the couple in front of us no longer occupies those seats?
The jollier couple still sits across the aisle.

The Strauses will be here Christmas Eve. Christopher
will again bring his almond pineapple appetizer—
he doesn't dare bring anything else, for fear of disappointing Mo-mie.

Augustana is being asked to be "reconciled"
to the gay/lesbian community. We've had outside speakers.
In January, we'll vote. Some people are very upset.
I fear it will tear us apart.

What do you think of your new Mayor?

January 1992

This is our thirteenth straight day of rainy, foggy weather.
Christmas was lovely: bright and sunny.

Stuffed peppers are cooking in the kitchen.
They were only nine cents each this week at Dominick's.

Last night we went to the Lyric production of *Madame Butterfly*.
Catherine Malfitano was wonderful as Butterfly—
I filled three tissues with tears.

It's hard to believe Peter will be 35 this month.
That was my most depressing birthday—
I thought my life was half-over.
Dad brought me a chocolate whipped cream cake.
Nothing ever tasted so good.

February 1992

My back has been hurting since January—
at 63, I feel like I'm falling apart. I should be more understanding
of Mo-mie's failings at 86. I doubt I'll make it to that age.

The days are longer, but not brighter. It was foggy in Beverly Shores—
I took a walk on the beach and felt like I was in a Monet.

Saturday, we heard a noise coming from the wetland area
and fifty red-winged blackbirds flew over our house.

Did you know Superman was born on Feb 29th? WFMT just announced it.

The Olympics are over—I watched when I could.
It was hard to see the falls.

March 1992

After a sunny day, a thunderstorm hit at 7:30,
just as I was finishing my last appointment.
It rained hard, then stopped. I do worry
about that hole in the ozone; we've had such strange weather.

I've enclosed an article about Ambrose Bierce—
I never knew San Francisco was such a vibrant city in the 1860s,
when Chicago was a muddy little place
on the banks of Lake Michigan. Tomorrow is election day—
I hope Carol Moseley Braun beats Alan Dixon.

Did Kris tell you a bluebird family nested in David's bluebird house?
They had five eggs and produced two fledglings.
I love bluebirds—and hardly ever see them.

April 1992

It was too cold to go birding this weekend—
instead, I sat in my kitchen rocker and watched the birds in our yard—
a kinglet, a downy woodpecker, several goldfinches,
plus the usual juncos, chickadees, and cardinals—

oh, and the wood thrush in back, such a sweet, shy bird.

Yesterday, we met Peter at the Medici for breakfast.
Matthew currently has a "crush" on me,
though I can't explain why. I even had to take him to the potty—
I tried to tell him Grandpa was better at that than me.

It hardly seems possible that tomorrow is May 1st.
In North Dakota, young men put May baskets—flowers and goodies—
outside the door of the young lady they have a fancy for.
The Communists gave May 1st a different meaning.
For us, I hope it turns warm.

May 1992

I'm defying the weather and doing spring tasks—
planting lettuce and basil, removing the plastic
from the side-porch door. It has to be warm one of these days.

I'm glad you called Thursday; we didn't know the violence was spilling over
to so many other cities. The verdict was wrong.
Fifty-nine bashings and they blamed the victim?
America is such a great and such a crazy nation.

I recently finished a fine book, *Burger's Daughter*
by Nadine Gordimer, a South African story.

I'll give it to you NEXT MONTH. I hate to think that soon,
our long-awaited trip will be over.

August 1992

The rainy summer has produced lots of bugs—
snails, slugs, earwigs. An earwig even fell into my Manhattan.
And I picked out fifteen cutworms from around my marigold plant.
They were happily eating it to pieces.

I'm slowly reading James Michener's *Alaska*, in preparation for our trip.
Eleven hundred pages of small print. He covers *everything*.

It was wonderful to meet Rachel so soon after her arrival—
a half day old. Peg's labor was short, she didn't even look tired.
Matthew helped her get settled in the delivery room,
a nice change from thirty years ago
when your siblings were whisked away for seven days.

Did I tell you we hung your wind chime in the Norway pine?
I can hear it when I sit on the upstairs porch.

P.S. I made one of your recipes today—a tomato, onion, cheese sandwich.
Very good.

September 1992

Twenty-eight years ago tonight, I was sitting outside on our stone stoop,
upset my labor hadn't begun. I'd been to the OB man that morning—
there were no signs. Then, on the 17th, there were stirrings of your arrival.

Over the next several days, I must get winter clothes out and ironed—
both to take to Alaska and to have ready for our return—
alphabetize last year's Christmas cards,
and consolidate my houseplants so someone can water them.
I'm working up the nerve to ask John.
I know he'll do it, but it will make him anxious.
Sheila's plants have died, and he blames himself.

Wednesday, I drove to a Grundig Radio shop on the north side
to buy a small short-wave radio for Dad for his birthday.
I think he'll like that, as he often listens through the night.
His 65th birthday will be quiet.

October 1992

The day we left Chicago was beautiful—I hated to leave
the still-blooming cosmos, zinnias, and geraniums.
Now we're in Anchorage, for three days, exploring the city.
They had an 8.6 earthquake in '64. Parts of the city slid away
on "boot leggers clay." They re-built cautiously.
Yesterday, we went to a movie simulating the quake.
I was anxious, as the seats shook us about.
In the cemetery, the Native Alaskans use whalebones
instead of headstones. In the Russian cemetery, near Homer,
the graves had picket fences around them to take the place
of Athabascan Spirit houses. We've seen calving glaciers,
eagles, a moose. There is too much to take in.

October 1992

I'm still racing to catch up on post-trip tasks.
We got home late on the 15th and I had a full workday on the 16th.
Mercifully, Dad allowed me to cancel the NYT while we were away.
He's never done that before.

The opera season began last week. We saw Rossini's *Othello*.
It's different in plot from Verdi's and Shakespeare's.
The bel canto was WONDERFUL.

Play Reading is tonight: *Awake and Sing* by Clifford Odets.
It's about a dysfunctional family. Dad has a role.

The Golden Lady in Jackson Park has been re-gilded and looks gorgeous.

I'm excited that Toronto won the World Series.

And John did fine with my plants.

November 1992

This won't arrive on time, but Happy Thanksgiving.
The treat is for Advent. I'm nervous that Christmas is so close—
my overseas letters are done, but I'm only up to the C's on my regular list.

Yes, the election results pleased us.
I'm glad they've had to add bathrooms to the main floor, for the women.

Last week, I saw my pulmonary specialist—
he said my "pneumonia" was gone. I wish I'd known I had pneumonia.
I could have at least taken a day off.

I'm still having trouble adjusting to changes in the *New Yorker*.
I was used to fiction following Talk of the Town.
Now it seems to go on and on, after the main article.

Off to fix hot dogs for supper—I'm getting off easy
because of our late lunch with Marcella.

January 1993

How can it be two weeks since you left—
the time has gone so fast. Last week,
Mo-mie was hospitalized for pneumonia and pleurisy
but is now better and has no blood clots.
Her broken pelvis is still painful.

Wednesday, I made a Thai fried chicken recipe that called for fish sauce,
NAM-PLA. Mr. G's didn't have anything by that name.
I used Oyster sauce, which I had.
But now I'd like to replace that, as I finished it.
Can you recommend a replacement?

I finished reading *A Thousand Acres*; it was good—
though I had hoped, by the end, someone's life would turn out happy.

How are your plants doing?
Mine are experiencing strange deaths.

March 1993

I wish you were here tonight. It is beautiful, with snow.
You wanted snow at Christmas and it only rained.
Now, on the Eve of Spring, we've had lots.

Roger Norrington conducted symphony last Saturday.
He doesn't use a score or podium. He wants to be "egalitarian"—
there was such a rapport between him and the orchestra.

Yesterday, I made a chocolate cake for Coffee Hour
and it separated down the middle, like the San Andreas fault.
I was ashamed of it. But Eric Albright went back for a second piece.
I could have hugged him.

We saw a production of *King Lear* earlier this month.
I kept trying to compare it to *A Thousand Acres*.

Are you getting any hummingbirds at your feeder?

April 1993

Our yard is glorious with daffodils, tulips, and warblers.
The trees have tiny green leaves. We'll be at Kristin's
the second week of May—I hope her baby waits until we get there.

This stationery is from a conference you and I attended with Dad.
Do you remember that? I think you left a pair of shoes at the hotel.

I loved your Easter card. I made something similar for Barbara
for secretary's day. I'm not sure she "got it"—
maybe she'll discover the "re-cycling" over the weekend.
Barbara's always teasing me for writing case notes on old greeting cards.
I hope my files are never subpoenaed—
though the judge might get a laugh.

May 1993

It's a beautiful spring day in West Virginia—
sunny, flowers in bloom, warm enough
to have windows open—but no baby cramps.
And our week is half over. This morning,

we went with Kris to her doctor's appointment—
and listened to the baby's heartbeat.
On the way home, we stopped at McDonalds.
Andrew recognizes the "M" of the arches as standing for "Mother."

We were hoping to take David fishing yesterday
but a storm developed. Instead, we made hash browns.

If Gloria Steinem's book did all that for you,
maybe I'll add it to my list. Right now,
I'm reading *Pigs in Heaven* by Barbara Kingsolver.

July 1993

It's hard to believe summer is a third over and days are getting shorter.
The weather has been miserable—we aren't flooding,
like it is in Iowa and Wisconsin, but it rains every day

or every other day. My dahlia was being devoured by snails.
I hate to use pesticides, but I sprinkled some of the powder
and now there are fifty dead snails around the plant.

Last weekend, we went to the mall in Michigan City.
I got paired with Matthew—there was nothing to do but ride the trolley
around and around. The driver kept urging us to get off at every Toy Store.

We can't wait to see you at the baptism.
We've called Dee a few times. She's missing Dolf,
but doing ok.

August 1993

I got home from work last night, just as a storm was coming through.
I spent an hour running from window to window,
wiping sills, then re-opening windows, as the storm abated.

The talk we had when you were here was special.
I had thought, with my career, that I was different from women
of my generation. But the message you received
was that my career was second class. It certainly was,
money-wise. I was embarrassed to see my earnings when I applied,
last week, for social security.

October 1993

It's almost two months since we saw you. Time is such a blur.
The rest of the summer was hot (briefly)—
then cold and wet. The coldest September on record.

It feels strange to be 65. I'm glad no one at LSSI knows—
I'd like to work a few more years. The purple top you sent is beautiful—
I love the color—and it fits perfectly.
Polly treated me to lunch (squash soup with pieces of apple)
and a movie, *The Age of Innocence*, for my birthday.

Last week, Dad and I attended a reception at the Field Museum
for the new U of C president. An impressive setting:
the new dinosaur was in place.

Right now, on WFMT, the *Verdi Requiem* is playing.
Polly dislikes the Verdi. She prefers the Fauré and Brahms.
I must look into those.

November 1993

The weather has been so pleasant, it's misleading me
into thinking Christmas isn't around the corner.
I thought I was doing so well with cards. Then I hit the "S's."
There are over twenty—and most require a note.

Last month, I attended the Homecoming Service at Trinity Lutheran.
I don't know why so many of their current members are afraid to attend.
I had no qualms; the area is well maintained.
I took pictures of the altar and baptismal font my parents gave,
in the forties, when the church was built.

Dad and I had a lovely time in Door County;
on Saturday, we went to a Karaoke Bar. Jerri and I
sang *Sentimental Journey*—to great applause.
Jerri harmonized and we did sound pretty good. Mainly,
we laughed and had a good time. We needed that.

January 1994

The sun was warm and bright when we got up.
We could almost have eaten on the upstairs porch—

but we settled instead for a patch of sunlight downstairs
where we could watch the birds. Just now,

I rescued the green windchime that was lying in the snow,
beneath a tree. We missed you at Christmas—

Betty and I went to Rockefeller. It felt good to be tranquil
for an hour, then we repaired to the house for champagne

and dinner—duck stuffed with prunes and apple,
the way my grandmother used to fix it.

I'm enclosing an article about New Year's Day Traditions.
You were in style eating beans and rice. This week

we're having Leonard over for Lutefisk. Dad and Leonard
will float into the New Year on melted butter.

February 1994

The weather has not been pleasant. Today, it was icy
when I walked to LSTC. At 5, it poured. I was soaked

when I got home—shoes, slacks—and made chili
for supper, an antidote to the cold.

Last Sunday was Ray Borling's funeral. He died two days
before his 90th birthday. You might remember Ray—

he always poured coffee at church. I finished
Their Eyes Were Watching God—it was wonderful.

I'm always sad when I finish a book. *Ms.* Magazine had an article
(years ago) about Alice Walker finding Hurston's grave.

What do you think of the changes to the *New Yorker*?
I find little of interest anymore. And I no longer understand the cartoons.

March 1994

Last Friday was grim. It snowed over twelve inches—
I had to pay someone to help shovel out my car.

But then your call came, with your wonderful news.

Our party on Saturday was a success.
Three people asked for my chicken recipe. Even the salad was a hit—
though the dressing was only oil and vinegar.
After dinner, we played ping-pong. I haven't been so physically active
since climbing to the top of Bald Knob, last August.

I just realized you'll be on the train on 4/21.
That's your engagement anniversary.
Your years in San Francisco have been rich.

WFMT is having their spring membership drive.
They keep reminding listeners that a NYC station has given up
and gone to heavy metal, and a SF station
might do the same. Is that true?

March 1994

Spring came today. The morning was warm and sunny;
the afternoon, cold and grey. Snow is forecast for Tuesday.
Winter won't let go.

This week, I had two Family Court appearances,
where I had to testify. I don't enjoy that; I'm glad the week is over.

The Olympics were fun to watch—I would have given Kerrigan a gold,
but I liked the gold winner, too. Jansen was delightful,
skating around with his baby daughter.

Have you ever seen Wendy Wasserstein's
Uncommon Women and Others? Play Reading produced it.
I was Susie Friend—an obnoxious senior.
My college years were nothing like that. Were yours?

Augustana is doing a series now on Death, Dying, and Grief—
it's good but it runs *four* Sundays.

May 1994

I got as far as the heading yesterday—then went to buy geraniums.
My trunk is a gorgeous flower bed.

Your cottage sounds wonderful.
I love that it's in a garden with flowers and trees.

Wednesday, I treated myself to a diversion for lunch—
Heaven on Seven in the Garland Building on Wabash.
It's noisy and popular. I had the gumbo soup.
Nineteen varieties of hot sauce sat in front of me on the counter.

Marcella's brother died in April. She was driving through Iowa,
on route to Wyoming, on that hot windy Tuesday
when you were here. Remember how gritty the air was that day?
In Iowa, the newly plowed fields left dirt flying everywhere.
It was typical, she said, of the dust storms she remembers,
years ago, in Dakota.

June 1994

Yesterday, the first day of summer, was 85 degrees
with breezes off the Lake. WFMT played Vivaldi's *Seasons*
and Mendelssohn's *Midsummer Night's Dream*.

I hope all is well in your cottage. After you left,
I remembered the cokes you were to take, plus French books,
more crackers, etc. Glad your boxes arrived—
and with only one item broken.

The National Association of Social Workers is meeting this year
in Nashville. I've never gone; it sounds dull. But this one is tempting.

The $20 is to offset start-up costs: a dish drain,
some cokes, a bag of beans, or a splurge of some kind.

July 1994

A thunderstorm just blew through—
the neighbor's dog is barking and I'm not even in the yard.

I finished reading Deborah Tannen's *You Just Don't Understand*.
It makes sense regarding gender differences—
and certainly applies to Dad and me. Next is *Care of the Soul*.

This week WFMT aired someone other than Glen Gould
playing the Goldberg variations; there were fewer than Gould plays.
I don't understand that. Maybe the person skipped some.

I hope the French is going well. Do you want a renewal of *Mother Jones*?

John harvested his first tomato from his balcony today
and gave it to us. He was so proud of producing it.
Shelia was always the gardener.

August 1994

It's a lovely day—I'm treating myself to forty-five minutes at The Point.
The Lake is deep green, with rolling waves.

After this, I must go home and fix supper.
I bought too many veggies for the Ratatouille—
we've been eating zucchinis all week. I wish I could send you a few.
Tonight, we're having zucchini "crab" cakes,
topped with salsa. Do you want the recipe?

Margaret Torsberg died Sunday. She was 79.
I'm going to the funeral tomorrow, before work.

I think sitting at The Point does more for my soul
than reading about How to Care for It.

October 1994

It's 10 PM after a long and busy workday.
I'll welcome tomorrow when I have no meetings.
Wednesday, I went to my first computer class—
our office will be getting them soon.
I'm excited to be learning about "windows."

Mo-mie and Betty left today for Amana. Would you believe
they're staying at the same place we stayed in '69?
It's probably still filled with my father's cigar smoke.

Right now, on TV, I'm watching the Carnegie Hall Opening
with a new Italian Soprano singing like a bird and loving her songs.

Friday, we attended a celebration for the Oriental Institute—
they're raising money for a new wing. The event was a bit stuffy,
but it was fun to put on dancing shoes and perfume.

January 1995

Enclosed are the answers to the crossword puzzle
we did when you were here for Christmas.

The slow movement was Lento, not Largo.
The pianist was Peter Nero. I hadn't thought of him.

It rained many inches on Friday and Saturday—
if it had been snow, it would have been awful.

Instead, it was only depressing. Today was so foggy,
I could barely see the Unitarian steeple.

Wednesday, I went downtown for an exhibit featuring Hyde Park artists.
The first painting Dad and I ever purchased was by a woman,

E. Levy. I was pleased she was included in this show—
to know she is well thought of and still painting.

April 1995

Dad picked up one of my habits while in Egypt:
this stationery is from his hotel.
Last night, we watched *Death on the Nile*—
filmed at the Old Cataract—so I could see where he stayed.

We're all missing Mo-mie in various ways.
In Beverly Shores, we passed the cookie place—
normally, we'd have gone in to buy her something.

Good Friday was a holiday—we drove to the zoo
with Andrew, Anne, and Chris, but it was closed. All we could do
was look at the lion, tiger, and camel through the fence.

Last month, we had the dedication for our new LSSI office—
we gathered in front, said dedicatory things.
Then, with an evergreen branch, we sprinkled the building with water.

May 1995

Supper is over—whitefish, hash browns, broccoli—
Dad is doing dishes. What a week it has been:
tears, worry, perplexity, then relief and joy.
I'm sad about your separation but understand the reason.
We're proud of how you got through the week.

Sunday, I watched the Kentucky Derby, hoping the woman would win.
She did well but didn't come in first. Similarly,
the women's boat, Mighty Mary, made a good show
in the America's Cup Trials. We'll get there someday.
It takes experience.

The O'Meara house is for sale. The two ladies are in a nursing home.
They're asking $200,000!

June 1995

It's a warm Saturday night. I'm half listening to "Help,"
an old Beatles movie. It's zany, but I like the music.

Today was full and not at all boring. I woke at 5, coughing,
and went downstairs to the couch in the dining room
(so I wouldn't bother Dad). I could hear birds,
through the screen door, as I drifted back to sleep.

In the afternoon, Betty and I went to the Art Fair—
we browsed for two hours, then sat in the kitchen
eating strawberries, Breyer's vanilla ice cream, and deep-fried onions.
Luckily, Dad settled for a sandwich for supper;
I had no energy, or appetite, to cook.

The map from AAA arrived. We were able to locate Lombardy Avenue.
We're excited to plan our visit.

June 1995

It's been a difficult week. Tuesday, Bob Sands, a friend of fifty-five years,
died. The wake was Thursday. Yesterday,
a Marynook friend died, after a two-week illness. And today,
a client I've seen since '89 died. Too many deaths.

Tonight, after dinner, the kitchen sink wouldn't drain.
Dad and I spent an hour plunging. We'll have to call the plumber.

Thank you for your letter. I cried, reading your vignettes
about children. I wish Katherine Louise was real,
so we could sit on the porch together and watch the fireflies.
Filing for divorce is so final but, as you said, there's no reason to drag it on.

I plan to park at Midway and be at your gate when you arrive.

August 1995

I'm on the side porch, eating leftover Bangkok chicken
and sipping a Manhattan. I can hear tree frogs,
cardinals, the sprinkler—and the Rockefeller Carillon.
Vacation is over. I relished my two free Mondays.

We enjoyed our visit to Nashville—seeing you in your cottage.
Will you send me your recipe for carrot soup?

We missed the Wild Turkey Tour on the way home—
we'd forgotten about the time change—
but we did tour the Ancient Age distillery—
that was my father's bourbon of choice.

The beach in Beverly Shores is gone again—
the waves were pounding the boulders when we were there.
It felt like another world.

November 1995

We're in our cabin on the Mississippi Queen.
It's 74 degrees here. We missed the snow in Chicago.
We should be able to have a good time—
if we avoid discussing politics or evolution.
Maybe we can reminisce about the 50s.

January 1996

I'm keeping up with full-time work, but I'm tired
by Friday. Last weekend we celebrated
Peter's 39th, which makes me feel old.

At church, we're reading *She Who Is* by Elizabeth Johnson.
Tonight, we discussed Sophia—the Wisdom of God.
I wish you were here to help me understand it.
Memories of God (by Bondi) is more accessible.
Her feminist awakening comes slowly, through a process.

March 1996

I started shredding cases today—I'll retire, in June,
from LSSI. It's strange to read old records.
Some clients I've seen for thirty years.

Tonight, Dad and I attended a Fireside Chat at the Quadrangle Club.
Ramsey Lewis, a jazz composer and pianist, played.
I've never seen so many African Americans at the Q Club—
that was wonderful to see.

Yes, I'm familiar with the MCC Church.
There's one that meets in the next block, at Brent House.

I would be delighted if, someday, you had a special friend,
and we could meet her.

March 1996

Spring is slow in coming. I'm grateful for longer days,
but hate the cold. Last week was so windy,
there were fish on Lake Shore Drive.

Dad and I saw our tax man on 3/6, then treated ourselves to lunch
at a Chinese restaurant on Wentworth. The Hot & Sour soup
was delicious; I'm still too intimidated to try your recipe.

How did the dance in Greenville go? I had a hair appointment
on Tuesday; Sue helped me find Greenville on the map.

May 1996

The warblers are coming through—
they're beautiful. I haven't seen any kinglets,

however, and I love them. An Oriole
alighted on the back porch a week ago,

and Dad has seen Redstarts.
The weather is awful: cold and rainy.

Everything is late. People are depressed.
There has been no spring.

August 1996

Dinner is almost ready—round steak in a tomato-basil sauce.
Dad is sipping wine on the side porch.

By now, you are moved to Linden Avenue.
On the map, it doesn't look far from Vanderbilt.

Thank you for your package—
you remembered how much I enjoy getting the clothes you're tired of.
The shorts, I wore today; the shirt, I'll try on later.

Having all of you at my retirement party was special.
I wish I'd gotten up and made a little speech.

Janie and Lloyd took us out for dinner Monday night.
I had a fish called Tilapia.

Becky says hello; she asks about you often.

September 1996

I didn't get home from jury duty until 6:30—
then dusted, sorted the mail, and took a bath.
Dad is tutoring at the Blue Gargoyle.

This morning, I went to Vera's for my hair,
then to Criminal Court. They give us coffee, bagels, and cream cheese
while we wait for the proceedings to begin.
Today we heard from a detective and forensic specialist.
There are so many missing pieces—
I hope tomorrow's testimony fills some in.

Our group is congenial and mixed: Three Hispanics,
four whites, seven African Americans. During the breaks,
we play Gin Rummy & Crazy Eights. And laugh a lot.

September 1996

My 50th High School Reunion was last weekend.
We sat with Trinity friends, Friday, for the dinner.

Saturday, we went to the recently rebuilt (after a fire)
Arlington Race Track. The Park is lovely—
I've always wanted to take you there.

Dad and I each went with $20 to spend.
I came home with $28. He came home with $40.

Next weekend, we'll attend the 50th wedding anniversary
of a woman for whom I was Maid of Honor.
After high school, she got married, I went to college.

We've had little contact since. The celebration should renew
memories. And we'll meet her family—three sons.

October 1996

Thank you for the Oatmeal Body Soak—
I'll save it for January when I hate to take baths.

I finished *Cloister Walk* (I wish I could be that spiritual).
Midnight in the Garden of Good and Evil is next.

This week, I watched *Bridges of Madison County.*
Dad taped it for me. I also need to watch *The Great Santini.*
I won't like it—it's about a military family
with an abusive father—but it was required reading
for a professor at LSTC. I've wanted to see it for that reason.

My Power Rider has arrived and is now assembled in Peter's old room
so I can look out the window; the basement is depressing.

Betty spent last week in Beverly Shores—
Hershey stayed up every night with her nose pressed to the patio door,
watching the wildlife.

November 1996

Our trip to Larimore went well. We attended Sunday services
at Our Savior's, saw Grandma's little house,
which looks the same—down to the hollyhocks by the front porch—
visited the cemetery, and ate at the Dairy Queen
(with noisy high schoolers!). Dad and Shirley (his cousin)
looked at photos and did lots of remembering.

It's a busy time for me at church. I'm chair of Stewardship;
we do a pledge drive in November. I'm not depressed yet
in retirement. John is in Paris for two weeks; he is amazingly active for 80.

It's almost Advent—my favorite season. Enclosed
is our first printed Christmas letter. We have succumbed....

January 1997

We woke this morning to six inches of snow and more predicted.
Sunday, it was 69 degrees. Strange weather.

We loved seeing you in Kentucky. I hope your cold is gone.

My first meeting with the LSTC book club
(for wives and staff) is Monday. The book is Toni Morrison's
Song of Solomon. It's excellent. Next, we'll read *Emma*.
I think we have an ancient copy on very thin paper.
I hope I can read it without a magnifying glass.

Saturday, we're going to the Lyric Opera Ball.
Dad really wants to go. I will tuck myself into a corner,
as I don't have a dress suitable for the occasion
and have no intention of buying one.

Sally (from church) is going through the same thing you did.
I've invited her over to talk.

February 1997

The paper today said February is the worst month
for winter blues. At least it's a shorter month.

I'm glad to know my mother's cape is keeping you warm.
You gave her the name "Ya Ya."

Enclosed is a treat for Valentine's Day—
maybe you can enjoy a cup of soup at Bongo Java.

I started reading *Emma*. It's a bit tiresome,
but I'm glad to be reading it. Last night, I had a bath

using the Oatmeal Body Soak. I only used half,
so I have enough for another use. Did you give me

Different Daughters? I've read it now and found it interesting.
I'd like to write a piece myself someday. Maybe I will.

March 1997

It's been a cold weekend—in the 20s. I'm eager
for the temperature to edge up to the 40s.
I picked forsythia a week ago; it's easy to "force"
and is blooming now in the dining room.

Tuesday, I saw my new physician—
I've switched, for the convenience,
to the U of C. He took a history
of the past six months, thumped my chest,
and gave me an undated prescription
for acute infections. I go back in a year.

Last night, for supper, I made a spinach salad with lemon/oil dressing.
It reminded me of one of your creations.

October 1997

It's 10:45—late, even for me. Book club tonight was at Becky's.
We discussed *Coming Home*—an idealized account of romantic liaisons

during WWII. Next month, I'm the hostess for Peter Mayle's
Hotel Pastis. Corinne leaves tomorrow for France
and promises to bring me back a bottle of Pastis to serve.

I still haven't begun *To Pray and To Love*.
Maybe I'll put it on my night table and read a bit
when I wake up or before I go to sleep.

Did you tell me you recently purchased a new pair of jeans?
I should buy myself a new pair. I couldn't live
without jeans. I wish I could wear them every day.

December 1997

Good news—Betty was able to get four tickets to the Messiah
from the "friend of a friend" who works at LaSalle.
This means Peg and Anne can attend. Anne arrives
Saturday; she's been feeling Messiah-deprived.

This morning, I saw Dr. Schaff. He keeps telling me to
floss, floss, floss. But I find flossing difficult to do.
Maybe Dad can give me an electric toothbrush for Christmas.

Did I tell you Hershey had fleas? Betty put "bombs"
all over her apartment, then sat in Ruthie's screen porch for three hours.

We're still making our way through turkey leftovers.
Last night, we had turkey soup. Tonight, turkey tetrazzini.
Time to get back to cards. The Brokerings are next.

January 1998

It's been a quiet Sunday. We had waffles for supper,
Dad did dishes. I was glad, though I have nothing to be tired about.

This morning we had our annual meeting at church—
no problems; it was over in an hour. But no Bologna sandwiches either.

What do you make of the Clinton scandal? I hope he doesn't resign.
Other presidents have had sex scandals. I'm eager to hear

about your trip to Puerto Rico. What do people there say
about being independent versus remaining part of the US?
If you heard anything, I'd love to know.

February 1998

They say it's the warmest winter in Chicago's history—
even daffodils are blooming. But it's grey and rainy and depressing.

Tuesday, I had an echocardiogram—it was neat to see my heart
pumping away; the echo lady called it "vigorous."
But the doctor said my heart is compensating for my lungs.
I'm to be a "couch potato"—not even bike to the Point. This month,

I'm book club leader for *Midnight in the Garden of Good and Evil.*
The library downtown didn't have much on the author; it's his first book.
I wonder how the ladies will react to Lady Chablis.

Our doorbell rang today at 1:15 and it was Jackie!
I hardly recognized her. She was on her way to lunch with Mrs. C.
She said she'd come back later for a longer visit, but never did.

May 1998

I have one eye on the *Antique Road Show*—it's a fun show
and tonight's is broadcast from Nashville.

I'm still struggling to get used to my oxygen. The yards of tubing,
especially on the first floor, keep getting in the way
as I vacuum or water plants. But I do have more energy.

This afternoon I attended a meeting of the Hyde Park Historical Society,
held at Robie House. The grandson of Paul Cornell,
who founded Hyde Park, spoke about his grandfather—
a man of great vision who started the first park system;
convinced the IC to come as far as Hyde Park
(so people could commute to the city);
built two hotels; and started a monument business—
his company made the lions that are in front of the Art Institute.

Tomorrow, our interim pastor starts—
I bought a bouquet of flowers for her and put them in her office.

Did I tell you Peregrine falcons are nesting on the Unitarian steeple—
one is on the finial right now, straight as a soldier.

September 1998

I'm sorry summer is almost over. Despite the heat and humidity,
I love summer—flowers, the lake, long days. Soon

it will end. Thank you for coming home last weekend—
it was great to see you, and the "little people" love being with you.

I hope Sunday School is going okay and those boys don't keep fighting.
The Cubs have been our big stressors the last few weeks.
Sosa vs. McGwire, etc. Today they lost in after-innings.

The woman who made this notecard used to teach at LSTC.
She's 85 now and has a "friend" she lives with and who inspires her work.

I'm happy you have a friend. Did I get her name right?
She sounds very nice.

October 1998

I just finished a bath, using the Almond Bath and Shower Crème.
Remember when you gave that to me, many years ago?

For my birthday, Dad took me to a restaurant on Randolph
I've been wanting to try. It was full of young people on expense accounts.
The couple next to us was having a private wine tasting—
the man pulled out bottle after bottle from a bag at his feet.
Our tables were so close, they included us in a few tastes.

I'm recalling my weekend with you last year—
making lentil soup together, sitting on your porch,
giving out candy to Trick-or-Treaters.

Our annual Block Party, last Saturday, was at Quaker House—
so, no alcohol. The new people in the Coates' house rescued the event.
They hosted a pre-party (with alcohol).

November 1998

Today, we went to Kinko's to pick out paper for our Christmas letter.
I wrote it, Dad changed it. I didn't like his changes
and we had a fight. But we negotiated and now it is done.

I saw my pulmonary doctor yesterday—he feels I'm stabilized
and doing fine, though I hate getting so out of breath.

A strange experience on Sunday:
I was supposed to be at the Blums for Play Reading,
but my dinner with Neva (at the Medici)
was delayed. The public phone wasn't working,
so they let me use the phone in the kitchen.
I had a "senior moment" and dialed Polly's number instead of Jean's.
When I got home, Jean was inside searching for me,
sure that something bad had happened.

January 1999

It feels strange to write "1999." Nostradamus
said the world would end in the seventh month of 1999.
Be careful in July—or come be with us.
We'll go to the Point. What better place to perish?

New Year's Day was Lutefisk Day for us.
Leonard arrived an hour early—I entertained in grungy jeans.
Probably no one noticed. The fish turned out well.
I always stress about it since I only make it once a year.

I'm looking forward to all being together in June—
and to meeting Laurie! Will she bring her dog?

March 1999

John had an exhibit tonight at the Union League—
they dedicated the month to French culture
and chose his photos from France. Six French cheeses were served
and five different pâtés. Plus, cabbage dumplings.

Driving to the Loop was slow because of snow.
But Daley had the salt machines going—he knows
who voted for his re-election. The Blums also
braved the weather. John was happy and proud.

I can understand your feelings of loss over your old church—
I had a similar problem when Trinity closed,
though at least it is now a thriving African American church.
Betty and I hope to visit someday after Easter.

How is your practice of ten deep breaths a month going?
That would benefit my lungs. I'm trying it right now.

April 1999

Our lives feel so busy. I can't tell whether ADL's
(Activities of Daily Living) are taking longer

or what the problem is. But our March 12th party was a success.
I'd been apprehensive—not sure I could do justice

to a sit-down dinner for ten—but the food was fine
and people said they hadn't laughed so much in a long time.

I'm glad I rose to the occasion. Thank you for the NYC
postcard. I love The Cloisters. And I envy

your chance to see *Death of a Salesman*. I missed it
when it was at the Goodman. I should have skipped

Christmas cards or cookies. I did see *The Iceman Cometh*
with Brian Dennehy. He brushed right past me

when I was in line for a half-price ticket. How did Central Park
get an Egyptian Obelisk from 1600 BC?

May 1999

It was nice to chat on Saturday—though I'm sorry Dad and I
got into an argument. We've recovered since then.

Have you read *The Color of Water* about a Black man
whose mother is white and Jewish? Neva pointed out
(in Book Club) that he had a sweetheart from Hyde Park
whose father was white and Jewish and whose mother was Black.
It was K.R.! She's mentioned in the book.

Yesterday, Dad stepped on a thorn while trimming trees at church—
the thorn pierced his shoe and foot. Ed came to our kitchen to remove it.
He is a good neighbor, surgeon, and gardener.

I loved your dream about daffodils. They're one of my favorite flowers.

If you "E" mail Doug, please send my greetings.

June 1999

Thank you for your letter. You buy such quality notecards—
while I use scraps of paper and old stationery "inherited" from Mo-mie.

The visit with you and Laurie was wonderful. You two
share many interests—she'll learn about birds, you'll learn about plants.
If Laurie's parents ever come to Chicago for AGA
(she'll know what that means), we'd love to meet them.

I'm enclosing an article by Mary Gordon. She writes so lovingly
about pens and putting words on paper. I love
my green malachite Schaeffer pen with blue/black ink.
I don't keep a journal, like she does, but I do write letters.

This Sunday, we're hosting a cook-out for the Call Committee.
Dad is the organizer and says I don't have to do anything. We'll see.

July 1999

Your monastery card came today. What a lovely place
for a renewal of faith. I'm currently reading *Amazing Grace*—
in small snatches, so I can meditate on it. The enclosed

is for you and Laurie to enjoy a special fish dinner
in memory of your grandparents. Saturday,
Dad and I went to the market—Halsted and Randolph—
to buy shrimp & smoked chubs. Such a mix of people
buying plastic bags of fish. My mother and father
both took part in that tradition, until her arthritis,
in '63, made it impossible to come to the South Side.

I recently finished a book called *Naked Before God*—
by a former LSTC student. He had cystic fibrosis.
Two siblings had already died when he entered seminary.
It's beautifully written. He died last spring.

Chicago is gorgeous now with flowers, trees, and the "cows"
which maybe you've read about: 150 plastic cows
painted in whimsical ways by various artists. I love them.

August 1999

It's cool and rainy. Rain is needed. The coolness
tells me autumn is coming. I'd like to stop the clock;

add a few more months of summer. The enclosed check
is for the house—maybe buy an aluminum ladder.

I've treasured mine which Dad gave to me one Mother's Day—
better than any candy, flowers, or perfume.

By now you've received our itinerary for Germany.
The reunion will be bittersweet—probably

the last time most of us will see each other,
as we are all in our 70s. I called someone in NYC

about having oxygen over there, but I don't see
how I can manage that. The tank weighs sixty pounds—
it won't even fit in a taxi.

September 1999

Happy New Year! Sarah (next door) says that's the greeting
for Rosh Hashanah. Why do services start so late?
It sounds like an Easter Vigil.

The nights are cooler here and the days,
shorter. I hate the end of summer.
I love to dash outside without a jacket or a hat and gloves.
But I do like the seasons.

Last week, I biked to The Point and sat for an hour.
I hadn't done that in two years. It was wonderful—
but I didn't breathe well. Today, I drove.
I have many happy memories of lunches there with you.

P.S. Sorry the ribbon on this card isn't purple.

October 1999

The garden plants that I bring in to "winter"
are now inside and on their familiar window sills.

Winter is soon to be upon us. Your new house
looks cozy. What room is to the left of the front door?

Dining room? Or bedroom? Your neighbors
sound very friendly. I could never tell anyone to

"come over anytime" for Sunday dinner. The fenced yard is a plus.
I hope the squirrels don't eat all your pears.

Our reunion in Germany was lovely, though we were weary
when we arrived. We visited Check Point Charlie

and the Egyptian Museum, plus a Greco/Roman one.
The Germans sure did a good job plundering.

December 1999

We probably sent this same card last year,
but I love penguins. The Christmas letter is new.

I'm glad you bought yourself a new winter coat—
I didn't know London Fog made a jacket in purple.

Do you remember when we tried to find Emma Goldman's grave
at Forest Lawn Cemetery?
And the Haymarket Square Memorial?

Betty took a tour last week and found them—
she also found the grave of Bugsy Moran,
a Chicago mobster. The inscription on his tomb said:
"I do it any old way."

January 2000

My bottles of water still sit on the butler's-pantry sink—
there were no Y2K glitches with our water system.

I'll use the water for plants on Tuesday. It's nice to think
of you and Laurie planting bulbs in your front yard.

I hope they thrive. If I am not writing very well
it's because I have my hands on the wheel of my new Volkswagen.

It's the best present you could have given me.
I could take it to bed with me, like a Teddy Bear.

But it's a little too "bony" for that. Now I must prepare
for Book Club. I recommended *The Education of Little Tree*—

the story about a Cherokee child, age five,
growing up with his grandparents after his parents died.

Do you read Writers on Writing? I didn't understand the article
by David Mamet. I'm not sure what a genre writer is.

February 2000

We've had a fair amount of snow, but nothing
like what hit Georgia or South Carolina.
The backyard is beautiful. So is Woodlawn Avenue.

I'm sorry we missed Laurie's birthday. Next year, we'll do better.
I love the purple garlic paper Laurie's grandmother gave you.
Maybe I should start doing something creative with garlic skins.

Your tour of Fisk University sounded fascinating—
especially the chat with the 93-year-old woman
from the Harlem Renaissance. I wonder if she knew Zora Neale Hurston?
Their Eyes Were Watching God made a powerful impression on me—
you introduced me to her.

March 2000

I so enjoyed the weekend with you and Laurie. I loved
seeing your house; the weather was perfect;
the Bat Mitzvah, with Laurie's help, was instructive.

The trip home was easy. At Midway, I sat outside
to wait for the shuttle. It was that warm.
A 24-year-old man from Nepal sat next to me and we chatted.
He asked how old I was and was surprised when I said 71.

Yesterday, I reached into the freezer for an ice cube
and my hand went into water. Then I noticed blood
dripping at the bottom. The freezer must have stopped while I was away.
The only bright spot is that Dad called from Egypt. These two weeks,
when I thought I could hang out with friends,
are proving to be busy. I'm still trying to catch up
on newspapers. Laurie is smart to cancel. Once they're here,
I have to read them.

P.S. I'm using this paper because it's your color.

April 2000

I'm thrilled that you and Laurie will be here May 12th.
I'm already thinking about what I'll make for Friday dinner.
Would you like cream of sorrel soup and a spinach salad?

Betty and Hershey will be with us on Sunday—I could serve whitefish,
if you'd like that. Your visit will be the best Mother's Day gift
I could receive. Dad said you offered to take us to the Medici.
That's very kind but I love our dining room and would rather eat here.

How are your bulbs doing? Our yard has been beautiful
with forsythia, daffodils, and a few tulips that the squirrels didn't find.

On Ash Wednesday, Pastor Gorder gave each of us a potted bulb
that we were to "nurture"—as our faith—and bring back on Easter
in full bloom. I put mine on the back porch and a squirrel dug it up.
I guess I'll fail at Easter. I hope I nurtured you children better.
I certainly didn't put you out for the squirrels to attack.

September 2000

It's hot and humid—not good for my breathing.

I hope you and Laurie had a fine time in Memphis—
I look forward to meeting her parents someday.

This card is early but we'll be flying to Spain on the 17th.
It will be a long and tiring day. I'll wish I was at home
and able to wish you a happy birthday.

Thank you for the Bongo Java coffee—it's delicious.
And Dad loves his King Tut bicycling jersey.

Friday, we took the #6 downtown to the Pharaoh of the Sun Exhibit.
On the way home, we waited twenty-five minutes for a bus.
Luckily, it was one of Dad's patient days.

P.S. Did I ever tell you how excited Rachel was to sleep in your old room?

September 2000

This morning we had a three-hour bus tour of Barcelona—
Joan Miró and Picasso both have museums here.
We also visited the Gaudí church.
It's not finished, though Gaudí is dead.
I hope to take Dad to a Tapas bar for his birthday.
Regular restaurants don't open until 9 PM.

November 2000

I haven't written in several weeks. I love to write—
but fall jobs consume me, especially with limited energy.

Storms are now down and in place, porch furniture
is back in the basement, yard plants are inside.

Monday, I hosted Book Club. The book was *Life So far*
by Betty Friedan. We had a good discussion
about the feminist movement—how it affected our lives.

Unfortunately, it was so good they stayed until 10:30.
Dad was wonderful to wash dishes, while I put things away.

Stewardship has also eaten hours. We've had five cottage meetings
and Sunday was our "thank you" lunch.

Last week, I won a turkey raffle at the Lutheran Brotherhood Meeting.
I haven't heard from the man who is to deliver it to me.
Tomorrow I will try to track him down and find out his plans.

December 2000

We're getting ready for the Play Reading Holiday Party.
Dad cleaned the living room and will lay a fire.
I bought a ham at Moo & Oink—also, expensive dinner napkins
at the Hallmark store. I hate to spend $10 on dinner napkins.
But it seems to mean something special to Dad.

Yesterday, Jean and Susan and I met Leonard at the Medici for coffee.
Leonard brought each of us a bouquet of four roses to celebrate
his becoming a U.S. citizen. I'm not sure why he'd want to,
but he's been on the list for several years.

January 2001

It's New Year's Day. The sun is shining,

but it's cold, with lots of snow. I'm tired

of snow: walking, driving. It's hard on my breathing.

Dad is at Ray's watching football with "the boys"—

baby Henry (7 weeks) and Cosmo, the poodle.

The days are getting longer; that is cheerful.

February 2001

My Monday client said I'd smell Spring on the 7th.
I didn't smell it on the 7th but I did on the 8th.

It was fifty degrees and raining. Now the rain
has turned to snow. Our lives have been quiet.

Symphony, opera, a meeting or two. I've agreed
to a two-year term on Church Council—

I might regret it, but one thing I can do
is sit through a meeting and give an opinion.

This afternoon we're going to the Branson's for tea and pie.
Last week, a grackle came down our chimney—

Dad put a board up. It's surprising how much chipping
it did to the stone ledge. I'll show you—
next time you come home.

Milly Dordal, 1970s.

Notes

"September 1983" (page 13): The house where I grew up was located in Hyde Park on the south side of Chicago, not far from Lake Michigan. In September 1983, I was a sophomore in college (at The College of Wooster in Ohio) and living away from home. The name of the woman referred to in lines 6 and 7 has been changed. Alfred (line 10) was the son of a family friend.

"September 1983" (page 14): Polly was a good friend of my mother's. The name of the man referred to in line 5 has been changed.

"July 1989": The apartment referred to in line 3 was located in San Francisco. I graduated from college in 1986, lived at home (with my parents) for a few years after college, and then, in July 1989, moved to San Francisco. The young men referred to in line 11 are the sons of a family friend. Their names have been changed.

"August 1989" (page 16): The earthquake mentioned in this letter was later determined to be a foreshock of the 6.9 Loma Preita earthquake that occurred two months later. The woman in the coffee shop who "predicted" the August earthquake most likely had misheard a television news report about emergency preparedness training exercises (for in the event of a major earthquake) that San Francisco city officials were scheduled to conduct the very next day.

"September 1989": Kristin (Kris) is my sister. She and her husband Paul have three children: David, Andrew, and Elise. I also have two brothers, Andrew and Peter. Andrew and his wife Anne are the parents of Christopher (Chris) and Nancy. Peter and Peg are the parents of Matthew and Rachel. Several of these children (my mother's grandchildren) are mentioned in the book. The "mistaken identity" reference is to an experience I had on my first day of work as a receptionist in a San Francisco medical office. A woman walked into the clinic and asked if there was anyone there named Lisa. When I told her my name was Lisa, she said she wanted to talk to me outside and that I wasn't going to like what she had to say. It turned out, the woman had recently discovered that her husband was having an affair with a woman named Lisa who worked somewhere in the building.

"October 1989": Jackie was a friend and former neighbor of my parents. Ray is a public elementary school in Hyde Park; Kenwood is a high school. Marcella was a longtime friend of my mother's. The earthquake was the 6.9 Loma Prieta earthquake that occurred on October 17, 1989.

"November 1989": Leonard was my mother's boss at Lutheran Social Services of Illinois (LSSI), where my mother worked as a family counselor. Leonard lived not far from my parents.

"December 1989": Lutefisk is a type of dried whitefish that, in Nordic countries, is typically served during the Christmas season. My father's side of the family is Norwegian. (My father's father emigrated to the U.S. in the 1890s.)

"January 1990": The ordination my mother is referring to was the ordination of Jeff Johnson, an openly gay man, who was ordained by First United Lutheran Church of San Francisco (where I was a member). At the time of the ordination, the national governing body for Lutheran churches (the ELCA) prohibited the ordination of openly gay ministers.

"March 1990": For six months, prior to moving to San Francisco, I rented a small apartment in Hyde Park and thus had a "landlady." Before that, I lived with my parents. The "tax appeal" is a reference to real estate taxes. My mother kept close track of how the Cook County Assessor's Office assessed houses in our neighborhood that were considered comparable to ours and, if there were significant discrepancies between the amount our house was assessed for versus what comparable homes were assessed for, she filed an appeal (an arduous process during the pre-internet days).

"July 1990": LSTC is the Lutheran School of Theology in Chicago and is where my mother worked part-time as a counselor up until her death in April of 2001. She was planning to retire later that spring. As previously mentioned, my mother also worked as a counselor (part-time) at LSSI, the Lutheran Social Services of Illinois. The reference to "CD tapes" is, of course, an error, but I let this error stand because it illustrates the challenges of transitioning to a new kind of technology.

"August 1990": Peter is my brother and Peg (in the letters) is his wife. Larry was one of the ministers at my parents' church in Hyde Park (Augustana Lutheran Church).

"September 1990": In 1977, my mother used money she had inherited from her father, who died in 1974, for a down payment on a summer/weekend house in Beverly Shores, Indiana. My mother insisted on buying this house in her name only because, when she and my father purchased the Hyde Park house in 1964, my mother's name was not considered necessary on the deed.

"May 1991" (page 33): Henry Russe was a friend of my parents (through church and the neighborhood). He was also a medical colleague of my father's.

"May 1991" (page 34): My parents purchased their Hyde Park house in 1964. The previous owner had rented out different sections of the house (while living there herself). One of those renters was Sheila, who lived in one of the two third-floor apartments and who continued to live there after my parents purchased the house. When Sheila married John, he moved in with Sheila. The house did not have a separate entrance for renters; Sheila and John entered through the front door and walked through the house to the third floor. After Sheila's death, John continued to live in the apartment.

"July 1991": As previously mentioned, LSSI is the Lutheran Social Services of Illinois, and Larry was one of the pastors at my parents' church (Augustana).

"August 1991" (page 39): As previously mentioned, Peter and Andrew are my brothers.

"October 1991" (page 41): The phrase "freed slaves" is problematic. It is more accurate to say "freed people." I kept my mother's original language here because the phrase "freed slaves" was likely the "norm"—problematic as it was—back in 1991.

"November 1991": Talman was a Chicago-based Savings and Loan that was affected by the economic recession of the 1980s.

"December 1991": Mo-mie was my mother's aunt. Betty (mentioned in later letters) was Mo-mie's daughter and my mother's cousin. The "Christopher" mentioned in this letter is a family friend, not my nephew. Augustana is the name of the Lutheran Church my family attended in Hyde Park.

"January 1992": My mother died at the age of seventy-two; at thirty-five, her life was actually almost half over.

"May 1992": The verdict my mother is referring to is the acquittal of four white police officers charged in the 1991 beating of Rodney King.

"October 1993": U of C is the University of Chicago.

"November 1993": Trinity Lutheran Church was located on the west side of Chicago in the neighborhood of Austin, where my mother grew up, and was the church she and her family belonged to. Austin was a predominantly white, middle-class neighborhood up until the 1970s, when Black, middle-class families began to move in; by the 1990s, the neighborhood was predominantly Black.

"January 1994": As previously mentioned, Betty was my mother's cousin. Betty and my mother were very close and, in many ways, were more like sisters.

"March 1994" (page 65): The news my mother is referring to in line 3 was my acceptance into an MA program in feminist theology at Vanderbilt University.

"May 1995": My mother is referring to my separation (and eventual divorce) from my then-husband after I realized I was a lesbian.

"January 1996": My mother worked full-time the last nine months of her employment at LSSI.

"March 1996" (page 80): MCC is the Metropolitan Community Church, founded in 1968. MCC was the first church to perform same-sex marriages and was on the forefront in the struggle for marriage equality.

"March 1996" (page 81): The dance my mother is referring to was a lesbian dance I attended with a friend.

"August 1996": My mother retired from LSSI in June of 1996. She continued to see clients part-time at LSTC up until she died.

"September 1996" (page 84): My mother switched to Vera for her hair after Sue retired.

"November 1996": Larimore, North Dakota is where my father grew up.

"January 1997": The name of the woman referred to in line 13 has been changed.

"February 1997": The full name of the book my mother refers to in line 11 is *Different Daughters: A Book by Mothers of Lesbians* (edited by Louise Rafkin).

"May 1998": The IC is the Illinois Central Train.

"March 1999": It's possible my mother meant ten deep breaths a day, but she wrote month. I'm not sure what practice of mine (from that time period) she is referring to.

"May 1999": For privacy reasons, I opted to use initials of a fictitious name in line 7.

"June 1999": AGA is the American Gastroenterological Association. Laurie's father and my father were both gastroenterologists. The Call Committee is a church committee charged with selecting a new pastor.

"August 1999": In 1949, my mother travelled to Germany to help rebuild a church located in the village of Herzogsägmühle which was founded in 1894 as a worker's colony for homeless men. During WWII, the Nazis used the village as a camp for people who opposed the regime. After 1945, Herzogsägmühle was turned into a church village offering housing to people suffering from addiction, mental illness, and/or homelessness. My mother maintained contact with the people she met on that trip and attended several reunions, including the 50th reunion in 1999.

"January 2000": The Volkswagen car was a twelve-inch toy car I had given my mother for Christmas. She had mentioned how much she loved the design of the new Beetle Volkswagen (which I was in no position to buy for her), so I purchased a toy replica for her. She loved the car so much she even took it to church with her one Sunday to show people.

"December 2000": Leonard was originally from Canada.

"February 2001": My mother died six weeks later, on April 7, 2001. This is the last letter I have from her (not including a postcard she wrote to me a week before she died).

Acknowledgments

A few passages in Part I are from my essay "My Mother Returns, This Time for Good" which originally appeared in the January 2022 issue of *The Sun* (Issue 553).

The Richard Rohr quotation in Part I is from Richard Rohr's Daily Meditation of Friday, November 12th, 2021 (Week Forty-Five: Christianity and Buddhism). The Daily Meditation is distributed by the Center for Action and Contemplation. This particular meditation, entitled "Being Present to the Presence of God," was adapted from Richard Rohr, "First Sunday of Advent: To Be Awake Is to Be Now–Here," homily, November 30, 2014 (Center for Action and Contemplation: 2014).

Photo: Beth Gwinn

Lisa Dordal is a Writer-in-Residence at Vanderbilt University and is the author of *Mosaic of the Dark*, which was a finalist for the 2019 Audre Lorde Award for Lesbian Poetry; *Water Lessons,* which was listed by Lambda Literary as one of their most anticipated books for 2022; and *Next Time You Come Home*. Lisa is a Pushcart Prize and Best-of-the-Net nominee and the recipient of an Academy of American Poets Prize, the Robert Watson Poetry Prize, and the Betty Gabehart Poetry Prize. Her poetry has appeared in *The Sun, Narrative, Image, Christian Century, Best New Poets, New Ohio Review, Greensboro Review, RHINO,* and *CALYX*. Her website is lisadordal.com.